Zebra's Yellow Van

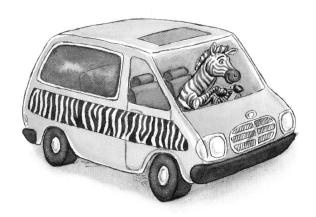

Written by Diane Phillips

◆

Illustrated by John Steven Gurney

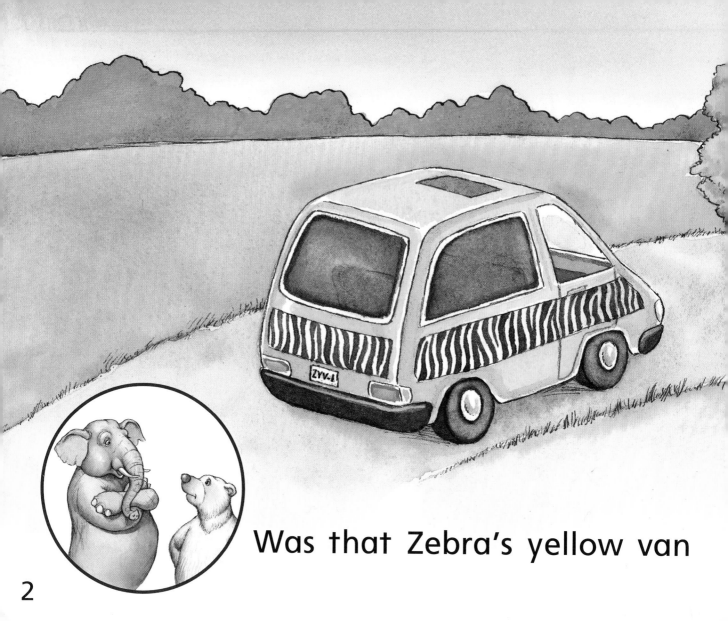

Was that Zebra's yellow van

2

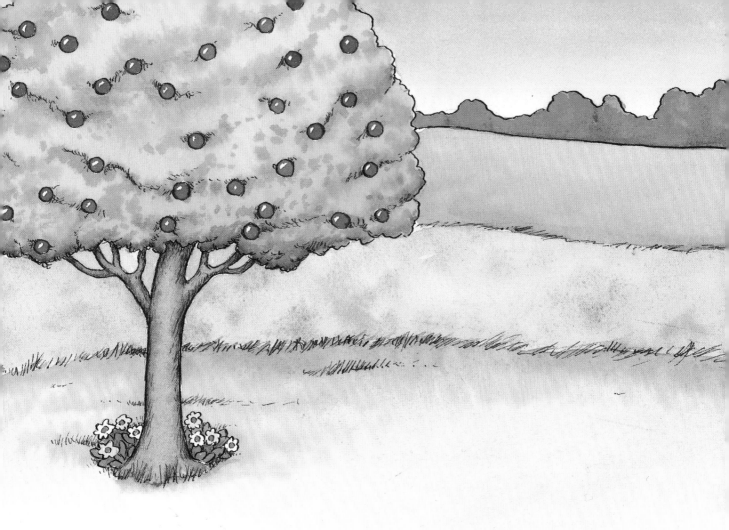

by the tree?

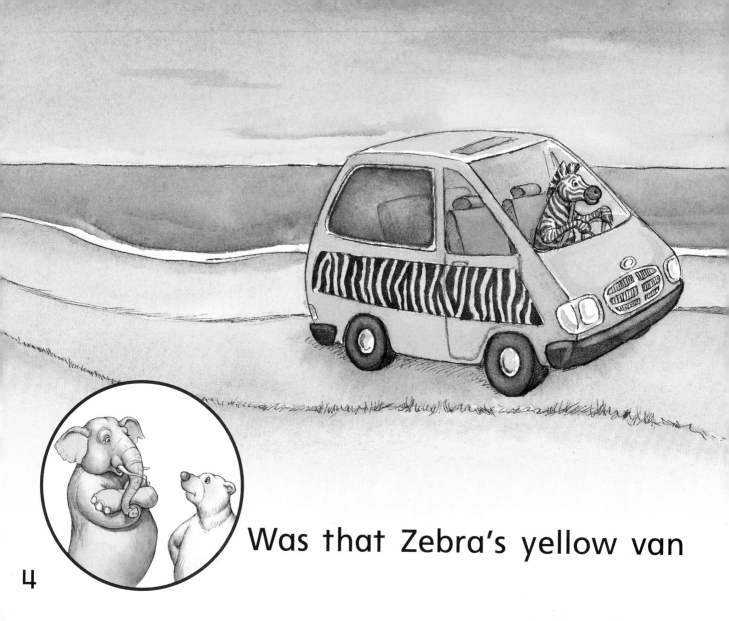

Was that Zebra's yellow van

4

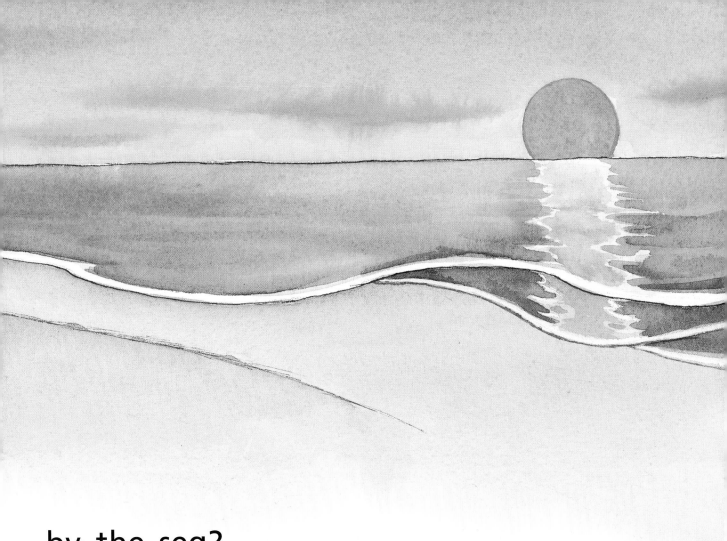

by the sea?

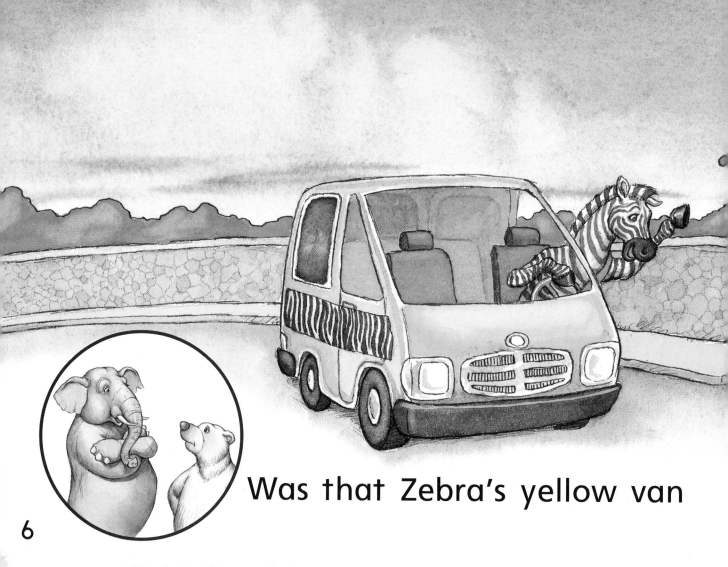

Was that Zebra's yellow van

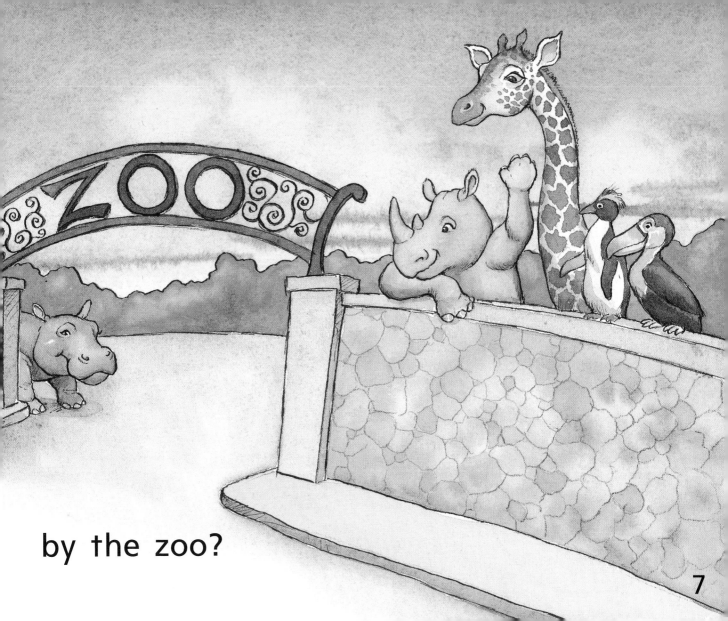

by the zoo?

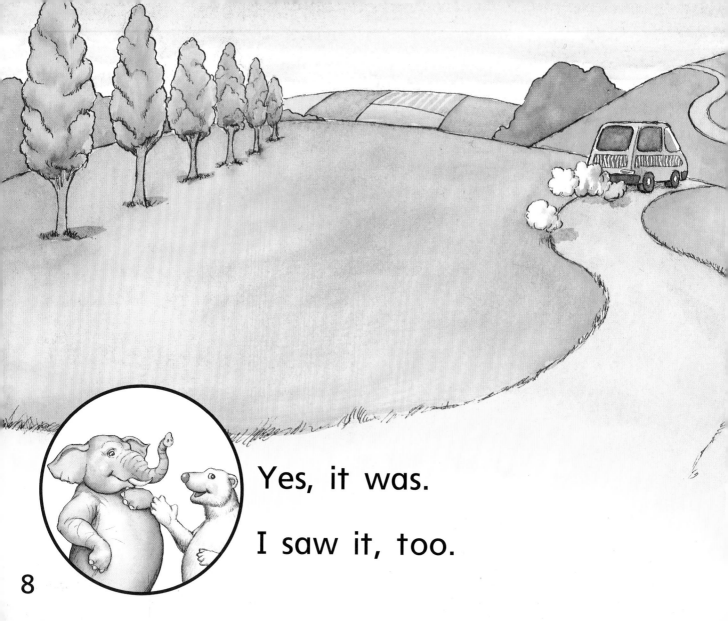

Yes, it was.

I saw it, too.